D1102046

The Healing Next Time

The Healing Next Time

Roy McFarlane

Nine
Arches
Press

The Healing Next Time
Roy McFarlane

ISBN: 978-1911027454

Copyright © Roy McFarlane

Cover artwork: Untitled 2006, (mixed media on digital image, 81 x 106cm) Copyright © Barbara Walker. Website: www.barbarawalker.co.uk

All rights reserved. No part of this work may be reproduced, stored or transmitted in any form or by any means, graphic, electronic, recorded or mechanical, without the prior written permission of the publisher.

Roy McFarlane has asserted his rights under Section 77 of the Copyright, Designs and Patents Act 1988 to be identified as the author of this work.

First published October 2018 by:

Nine Arches Press
Unit 14, Sir Frank Whittle Business Centre
Great Central Way
Rugby
CV21 3XH
United Kingdom

www.ninearchespress.com

Printed in the United Kingdom by:
Imprint Digital

To Maish
To love and be loved in return

Contents

New Millennium Journal

… they killed them

Gospel According to Rasta

God gave Noah the Rainbow sign, no more water but the fire next time.
James Baldwin, *The Fire Next Time*

New Millennium Journal

Addressing our individual and collective suffering, we will find ways to heal and recover that can be sustained, that can endure from generation to generation.
bell hooks, *Killing Rage: Ending Racism*

1999 – Parts of a broken man

the more a man has the more a man wants
—Paul Muldoon

i.

On Sunday, the preacher's speaking of revelation and repentance,
the end of the world is on the lips of news reporters.
Cults are spreading and in the basement of a computer department
they're preparing for the invasion of the millennium bug—
       we watch for the skies and miss the stones at our feet.

*

The family man is shooting a basketball, graceful
in motion and everybody's watching the flight of the ball
reaching its zenith, then beginning to fall. All things fall;
summer rain, falling from grace, the fallout
       of a sordid affair; the ball's falling.

*

Breadfruit, soursap, plantain. A Saturday morning ritual,
roles changed, the son takes his mother to a Caribbean stall
in Bilston market. She's not as strong as she used to be,
her breathing laboured, but she snaps the heads, digs out the eyes,
       yellow yam, sweet potato, dasheen.

*

       A daughter will be born soon, an olive branch
       for the family man treading water after storms ceased.

ii.

A nation hears no evil, sees no evil, speaks no evil. A son's blood,
a father's sweat and mother's tears will lead a retired judge
and three diverse men to inquire in towns and cities
of the racism that kills. And the rocks will hear and rivers speak
              of the death of Stephen Lawrence.

*

After hearing of the death of Grover Washington Jr,
the family man's falling asleep with his Walkman headphones;
between *winelight* and *come morning*, memories are awakened,
whirl of cassette tapes beginning the rewind of illicit love:
              just the two of us building castles in the sky.

*

Late meeting, lips kissing, hands feeling, fingers…
Her halter-neck top has been drawn over her head,
the night air touching her breasts, powdered
with a flurry of goosebumps, he's sucking greedily
              and it all begins again.

*

        A mother's sharing roast breadfruit, ackee and saltfish,
        with a warning: *please, set your house in order.*

iii.

There are no purple skies but the prophet Prince lives
to see his words come alive, as people *party like it's 1999*.
We could die any day. James Byrd Jr died the year before;
lynching-by-dragging, hate driving for miles in a pick-up-truck,
                    driving from century to century.

*

He's speaking at public inquiries, tongue heavy with injustice,
teeth grinding to the sound of another death in custody.
There's a bitter taste, he needs something sweet; later in a private place
her labia moistened by his tongue, she guides his erection deep
                    and voices are lost in each other's mouths.

*

He's singing gospels, praying repentance into the early morning,
following traditions from sunny islands, avoiding the tears
of his wife, who's dreaming of impending sorrows. The millennium arrived
drunk with Hogmanay, midnight mass, Kwanzaa blessings
                    and Prince alighted from the heavens in a purple robe.

*

A new job, but *the more a man has the more a man wants*.
He leaves doors unclosed, doors that ache in the wind.

2000 – There are no gods in the midnight hour

i.

2,000 doves of peace released into the new millennium, holy doors opened,
a Pope in purple uncovers the sins of the Church, kneeling in *mea culpa*,
praying for forgiveness by the beating of his breast; it takes three priests
to open the doors of St Paul's, so many doors to open, how many more
                  to begin a healing?

*

An out-of-town preacher draws a crowd and the family man's watching
the *fire and brimstone* bubbling in the orator's veins, the *sweet by and by*
sweating through his pores, as he looks them in the eye with hands raised high.
They're all running to the altar, clothed in guilt, hoping for healing and saving
                  by touching the hem of his Armani.

*

A mother's hands are over-ripened and seeping with eczema,
each finger bruised and darkened. The son takes cream and rubs
her hands; hands that worked hard, hands that scolded him
when needed, hands that took a hold of Jesus' hands, hands full of sweet love.
                  Now he's massaging her weary hands.

*

                  There are no gods in the midnight hour,
                  only porn and replays of Janet Jackson.

ii.

Anytime, anyplace, in a car Janet's voice tied them with the *Velvet Rope*
album cover on the front seat, CD playing, files and paperwork on the floor.
Secret lovers accustomed to the shape of each other, the folding, morphing
in confined spaces, the tightness, urgency. Janet duets with this affair,
whispering; *I want you now, I don't want to stop.*

*

The family man misses out on the Highland pipers and African drummers
at the funeral of Bernie Grant, a firebrand burning in the House of Commons;
the media tried to put out his flame after the night of fires when cities
became beacons of insurrections. Broadwater Farm rises
as the father of lost causes passes by.

*

A middle-aged white man cycles past the family man in the middle of Oxford
shouting *fucking nigger* in the air. The family man runs after him, drags him
off his bike... The truth is, he's still standing on the corner adjusting his suit,
watching him ride into suburbia, the village, unchallenged circle of friends.
He's always brushing these things off.

*

In his mother's kitchen, he walks in a silent rage.
She knows, and places her hand on his troubled heart.

iii.

The family man as the activist stands to address a group of police officers
in Hull—the home of William Wilberforce, a market town founded
by the monks of Meaux Abbey. He freezes; *May my tongue cling
to the roof of my mouth if I do not remember you,* Christopher Alder
               who died in police custody.

*

The family man will be caught up with dial-up-lines, kung fu films and MTV Base;
between May Day riots and Tony Blair being heckled at the WI. There's a virus
ILOVEYOU spreading, seeping out of Windows across the globe into a family man
sick with the delusions of love, a fever of lust in the summer of secret rendezvous;
              We have a special need, to feel that we belong.

*

A nation's greatness is measured by how it treats its weakest members.
Hands outstretched to help refugees will now be filled with vouchers
and hate for foreigners. The temperance of a nation drops below-zero
as the Arctic wind sweeps in thick snow and the millennium wheel freezes.
            The door is closing in the coldest winter.

*

           The door slammed on the London nail bomber quoting
           The Turner Diaries for terror poured on Brit(ish) streets.

2001 – When the devil comes calling...

Beauty is mysterious as well as terrible. God and the devil
are fighting there, and the battlefield is the heart of man
—Rumi

i.

They're waiting for the activist to begin a meeting. He's been waiting
for the kiss; so long apart from his lover the kiss can't be parcelled
for another day, the kiss you want to unwrap, a kiss so enticing that it pulls
at the tightly-wound strings. A kiss he needed to steal; he grabs, kisses her.
     A kiss that is caught by his manager walking in.

*

Waiting for a meeting to start, Jim's memories are stirred by the news of a bomb
outside the BBC. His large frame shudders; *there's always a warning,* 6 minutes,
21 people died, the bomb under the Rotunda and the bus he should have been on
all pock-marked and deformed. The next day with *Irish bastard* ringing in his ear
     he left work with a warning to take the weekend off.

*

Another session finished for the activist tackling racism in Bedfordshire,
making his way back to his family, resting at a service station, eyes drawn
to a television. A plane crashed into a tower—reality and disbelief collide—people
looking to each other for answers. *Oh my god, another plane hit, did you see it.*
     He leaves and drives under a falling fog of fear.

*

          There's an aftermath of blame and scapegoats,
          debris falling on the streets, falling everywhere.

ii.

Christ is the divine son, to others the prophet, and here in Birmingham
she's wearing a veil. They're spitting, swearing and tearing the veil away
as they beat and buffet her, telling her to go home as she jumps on the No. 11
back to where she was born in Handsworth—Brummie accent on the tip
                    of her tongue blending with the sweetness of her beliefs.

*

Jim's wishing for rain to wash all this madness away, like the musical rain
in Killaloe, County Clare, running into the ground where his family's buried,
the rain that fills the River Shannon. Rain that fell on the faces of rebels
who made O'Dea Castle a stronghold, rain that has swelled his family name
                    across the waters in times of potato famines.

*

Between meetings and conferences, the devil busies idle hands and lips,
they said they would never do it again but like an addiction they're sinking;
submerging bodies wet with anticipation, biting necks, clawing backs
and buttocks. Later the writing is on his back as the family man goes late to bed
                    wearing a t-shirt and feigning illness.

*

                    In the morning he'll rise, fresh suit, a suitcase filled with
                    Cornel West and bell hooks whispering *Ain't I a Woman?*

iii.

Oldham vs Stoke became Whites vs Asians from the terrace to the streets, leaving
Oldham burning all night. Blunkett was enlightened to the parallel lives of Oldham
and Bradford leading to riots but walked in the shadows, throwing human rights
out and dragging dark veiled bodies through a blind-folded court system
caught up in the glare of a *war on terror*.

*

Colour, culture Jim says *it's all the same.* The activist responds *Blacks have been
doing this for over 500 years, fucked over by slavery.* Jim rises, *and you don't think
Cromwell fucked us over, enslaved us?* The activist, *you guys were terrorists to them,
but walk into a shop and say nothing you'd be overlooked. But if you're Black or Muslim?*
Jim smiles, *Aye, the devil in the details.*

*

The family man stands in his suit on an outside basketball court,
he shoots, the ball hits the rim; *What's happening to me?*
He plays with the shadows, they mark him tight as he drives
to the board, misses, screams and throws away the ball.
The shadows follow him as he walks into the night.

*

He looks to the skies as the rain falls. Shelters
in a phone box and makes a call. *I need you now.*

2002 – What we do when things fall apart

i.

It's all for you, if you really want it. Driving to a country hotel the activist
and his lover are playing Janet Jackson. The heat causes a shirt to open,
a dress to peel away; the wind blows through opened bodies, he hugs
the bends and trails his finger along her lips. She opens her legs wider;
                    guess I'm gonna have to ride it tonight.

*

The activist and his lover arrive at a hotel coloured in Elizabethan splendor.
Sorry. Are you sure you've booked? The lovers and the lush green lawns change
into black and white. *There's no room.* The owner flustered, running around
like Buster Keaton; this silent movie becomes painful to watch.
                    I'm sorry. There must have been a mistake.

*

I just don't understand this equality crap, just pull yourselves up by the bootstraps.
The activist smiles in a training session. *Okay! Let's look at this further* but he wants
to strip him of his boots, beat him senseless, place a chair over his windpipe.
Now pull yourself up by the bootstraps. Holding a rose in a clenched fist makes you
                    bleed as much as the aroma that escapes.

*

                    The son is reminded by his mother
                    dem ave de handle and wi auld di blade.

ii.

Dudley becomes the epicentre of an earthquake. Two in the morning
locals in Lower Gornal are on the streets, an elderly lady peeks out
her bedroom window, *what's gooing un ower wench?* The neighbour responds
There's been an earthquake Mrs. B. Mrs. B, responds as if to flick a fly away.
            Earthquake? We dow do earthquakes round here.

*

Tupac has never known California love, but he knows the love of Wednesbury
and the boys who bleed from the plains of Bangladesh, loves Zidane, chips
and kebabs, joins in the chants of *Albion* on Saturdays. Tupac knows the rhythm
of hip hop, dreams of Audis and weed and ends the day with *Inshallah*
            when he's not running the gauntlet of *fucking paki*.

*

A friend of the activist steps off the tube shaking; sitting by a thick-set man
who rolled up his sleeves to show the ritual marks of the NF, C18 &
Nazi swastika. It's growing in the shadows; in the debris of the Twin Towers,
in the soil of Ground Zero, finding its target in the hijab, the foreign-speaking,
            dark-skinned, five-times-a-day-praying believer.

*

            Ronaldo and Brazil win the World Cup a fifth time
            Black guys cheering, having a Bud, *wassssup.*

iii.

Zidane was a royal prince on the courts of the football arena, Achilles
gloriously designed, unperturbed, untouchable. Watch him in the UEFA
Champions League Final score the greatest goal ever. Watch a mythical figure
glide past tackles, protect the ball, thread passes through the eye of a needle
carrying the duality of the colonised and the colonialist.

*

You need to get your boys on the van, now, warns a female youth-worker.
An anti-racism football game is not going well. Brown boys beating; white boys
red and bruised. *Who the fuck you calling a paki?* Tupac pins a boy down
by his throat; the activist awaits, leaves it hanging, squeezing the air out and then
he pulls them apart, *Boys, we need to go. Now!*

*

On Sunday mornings the skies are righteous, road quiet, calm in a world
where all things fall apart, the family man drives a seven-seater. A daughter
unfolds her favorite seat. Everybody has their favorite seat. The family man's
trying to hold it together, keep the engine running smoothly, watching
dials spin, bounce and turn at the turning of his key.

*

He's telling lies, they're telling lies,
Bush and Blair are telling lies and everybody dies.

2003 – And who will wipe away our tears

I imagine one of the reasons people cling to their hates so stubbornly is because they sense, once hate is gone, they will be forced to deal with pain.
—**James Baldwin**, *The Fire Next Time*

i.

No blood on the lintel of a church where the family man and his children
bring in the new year, but around the corner there's blood on the street;
Letisha and Charlene know nothing about revenge but are shot outside a party.
A mother waits outside a ward, one daughter dies, the other's fighting for life.
        Who will wipe away a mother's tears?

*

Black thinkers, activists, community tellers, a few white men and a woman
gather together to speak of killing rage in the city. But there's a rage, found
between the reports of victims of race hate and the failings of institutions.
Uncle Tom is thrown at a black officer, a chair is kicked over, a jacket grabbed.
        Voices raised and two black men are held apart.

*

The family man arrives home late. Accusations. Lies. Rage.
Front door slammed. A car driven at 80. He's propelled
by fury like a meteorite flying past solar systems,
missing planets. Only the gravitational pull of his children
        draws him away from the black hole of guilt.

*

        The family man has never known his birth father—
        it's not the path he would choose for his children.

ii.

His lover pleads, *come with me*. Kissing under the shelter of a tram stop
things look different in the electric glow of ads to far-off places.
And, for a moment he glows faintly with dreams of leaving, but the lives
of his children shine brighter and the years of his affair dull
                in the afterglow of an autumn night.

*

He drives beyond the city walls to the coast, into the hills and valleys
into the sprawl of the vales where you meet so-called innocence,
the harmless traditions of blacked faces, Darkie Day singing
Minstrel songs and gollywogs, harmless to *whom?* A constant offence,
                a continual reminder of the past.

*

African Liberation Day filled with images of Black kings and queens.
History and myths found in carvings and drawings, stories and speeches;
The activist embraces these narratives, feeds on Black pride, dances
in the knowledge; *until you have your own history, you will never know*
                who you are. He leaves alive and loved on this day.

*

                War everywhere. The US invade Iraq. Saddam's statue
                is toppled, and on an aircraft carrier, Bush smiles.

iii.

The activist is angry with God who walked hand in hand
with colonialism, watched and said nothing as Empires
took on his image. A white God who feasted at the table of supremacy.
A God who was nowhere to be found in the midnight hour. He understands;
         Dutty Boukman; Nanny of the Maroons and Nat Turner.

*

Another earthquake hits Dudley when the Muslim Association
submit plans for new mosque in Hall Street; the shockwaves can be felt
across the borough, a tremor felt across the BNP landscape; a shaking
that draws people nationally and locally to stand and demonstrate.
         Muslim mosque? We dow do Muslims round here.

*

A protest brings the activist face-to-face with *this is England,*
snarling dogs. He's walking home, the stench of a rotting ideology still pungent
in a new millennium, bulldogs sick with phobias prowling the street, foaming
at the mouth. The activist, fist clenched, filled with fear, waits, waits, waits,
         they cross over; he unclenches his fist.

*

         Mars makes its closest approach to Earth
         and Saddam is found crouching in an eight-foot hole.

2004 – When the ground shakes

See the world through the eyes of society weakest members and then tell
anyone honestly that our societies are good, civilized, advanced, free.

—Zygmunt Bauman

i.

Weapons of mass destruction could hit Britain in 45 minutes.
A dossier is sexed up, the BBC exposes the lies. A weapons expert
commits suicide. The Hutton Inquiry lies on the table, brushing past
the truths. Blair said he didn't lie but when they lie, people die.
                    Another report airbrushed, whitewashed.

*

In the land of Hugh Hefner, Larry Flynt and cheerleaders titillating,
the greatest gladiatorial sport breaks for the Super Bowl halftime show.
Janet seduces, scintillates, takes us back to *Rhythm Nation.* Justin gyrates,
tears off a part of her clothing leaving a breast exposed; *by the end of the song*
                    a black woman crucified, a white man forgiven.

*

Past the Angel of the North, Newcastle is the furthest northbound the activist
has ever ventured. On a grey mothball day, he steps off the coach, into a sea
of white, a city with no colour and here the 10% non-white makes sense,
here he treads alone, here he feels the weight, simmers in the discomfort
                    of whiteness, leaves the city.

*

                    Are you okay? Yes mum I'm okay. *Are you sure?*
                    Yes mum! *A nuh same day leaf drap it ratten.*

ii.

Outside the walls of Caernarfon, a man walks up to the activist—
and they made us bow to a child that would be prince. Bastards.
The spirit of Madoc still hangs in the air. Later in training he learns
that the *Welsh Knot* wasn't the only thing hanging around the necks
        of a people in the land of *foreigners, strangers.*

*

Do you know what happened 200 years ago? The activist sits brewing
listening to a speaker from out of town. *The greatest insurrection, the Haiti Revolution,
a country freeing itself of slavery…* he continues and a room
of angry black men are drawn in. *Freedom is not given, it's taken, we wrestle,
        we stand together and turn back the tide.*

*

The activist and a colleague visit the home of a victim. A white woman
talks quietly as her daughter watches *Finding Nemo;* everybody stares
at her heavily-bandaged arms. She asked *Am I dirty, mummy?* I said *No darling.
At school they call me a dirty darkie.* I found her in the bath scrubbing her skin.
        Silence takes the weight of the tears in the room.

*

        A flash flood in Cornwall washes cars out into the sea.
        A flood of outrage washes over the activist every day.

iii.

The activist falls in love again, finds peace walking along the Thames;
they paint a picture in the moving swirl of tourists, dip in the heat and damp
air of desire. A painting that spills into the evening, daubs the walls
of a hotel bedroom, bodies coated in the gloss of each other
                    saturating the bed they fall into.

*

For the delicacy of cockles, for the rhetoric of too many migrants,
for the easy pickings, 23 Chinese people will rake a living in the sand
and won't see the rising tide sneaking in, the new slave labour swelling
across Britain. Dying on the shores of Morecambe Bay, the invisible, the vulnerable
                    inhabit our nights, live in our shadows.

*

The Boxing Day tsunami will be remembered, and for the family man
the displacement of waves swelling over the years. There's no defence:
cinema tickets, hotel reservations, rumours in the air, whispering phone calls.
A tsunami swells in the heart of a wife who has loved and given all.
                    All a family man has is washed up in the garage.

*

                    A mother's door is always open; as he walks through
                    she shakes her head, but he smells *toto* cake in the air.

2005 – Every second counts

i.

A new year, betrayal ringing off the bare walls of a one-bedroom apartment.
Picking up the ripped copy of Ralph Ellison, *Invisible Man*, the activist's
thinking of lost chapters, the soprano off-tune, the tear in a masterpiece,
the artefact smashed into a thousand pieces, and he hears her last words:
              You'll never know how it truly feels.

*

Years before leaflets blew around Weoley Castle: *asylum seekers*
stealing our services. A closed medical centre bought by Iraqis
became the home for communities—four times the wolves of hate
set alight the hopes of a place called home. Help from locals
              couldn't bring them back again.

*

The family man returns home to sign cheques, pick up clothes; the kids are away.
She greets him cordially, she's drinking. He notices the lace bra through her blouse,
her wrap-around skirt. *Why? Why? What did I do?* She beats her fist into his chest,
he holds her close, she unravels, blouse opens, skirt unwraps. They make love.
              After all is done—*Leave please, leave now.*

*

              36 years and the IRA end their armed campaign,
              4 suicide bombers begin theirs.

ii.

In the summer, a tornado in Kings Heath: a lone white man wants to clean up
the debris of hate. Wearing glasses, a tweed jacket, with a vice for smoking,
he draws together nuns, Muslims, community workers, elders and young people
over a weekend. He's a disciple of Martin Luther King, bringing
                    hope and healing during debates of despair.

*

The streets whisper that a black woman has been raped, local radio
grabs the news with fever. Hate ferments in the pot of rumors, half-truths,
the desire to affirm our prejudice. The community mass outside
the accused shop. The woman slips through our hands, into myth,
                    into the night, leaving anger behind.

*

Searching for an answer for the flood outside, here on hallowed ground
behind holy walls, a gathering of the good, the bad and the unloved.
An ex-gang member speaking for the anger outside: *these are the children
you threw out of these holy buildings, out of schools, out of your yards*
                    and on the eve of rioting they came knocking.

*

                    This sanctuary of community cohesion
                    wasn't made for the fire that was to burn.

iii.

It rains anger all night, rains fire, rains division,
pours down streets, seeps into shops. It pours down
on Isaiah Young-Sam returning home from the cinema, and when
hostilities end, they find Isaiah dead, beached on the streets of Lozells.
               The family man calls home to his children.

*

Crimes against humanity. Expressing *deep sorrow* is the best Tony Blair
could utter; switch channels. A documentary about the Ku Klux Klan
don't you know that they are cursed and *the sons of Ham a servant of servants
shall he be unto his brethren;* switch channels. Hurricane Katrina, black people
               looting, white people finding; switch, switch.

*

The radio chants *Warning of Gales in Thames, Dover, Wight…* Tonight
he stands by the window looking across the yard backing onto other flats,
most light swallowed in the darkness. He's tuning into childhood memories,
safe in his mother's bedroom, mum preparing psalms before they go to sleep;
               Dogger, Fisher, German Bight

*

               Lives were lost, love was lost —
               an extra second brings this year to an end.

2006 – New wine in broken vessels

*Some victims as more worthy of condemnation than others
is unforgiveable – and a betrayal of anti-racism itself*

—**Yasmin Alibhai-Brown**

i.

His lover finds a secret note she didn't write—*she said you'd never be faithful*
and walks out the door. He's watching Janet's 'I Get Lonely' video into the night,
Janet walking seductively down a corridor, opened blouse *begging you to stay,*
caressing a mannequin from behind. He's wishing his lover was behind him,
                    wrapped around his body.

*

The year before, Anthony Walker was rushed to a hospital with a pick-axe
in his head. The division of colour remains. The activist had walked, marched
and driven around the country and found nothing united in this Kingdom.
He thumps the walls in an elevator, doors open.
               He walks into the conference: United Against Racism.

*

A manager thanks him for all the work he's done, but funds are coming
to an end. *You kidding me, seven years and they're closing us down.*
Seven years to rewrite centuries of hate. Seven years to plant seeds of hope.
Always waiting for riots, or a Stephen Lawrence, don't they ever learn?
               A table is turned upside down.

*

               Hate was easy, loving was hard, hate laid down
               like a rotten fruit, but loving needs to be nurtured.

ii.

Zidane leads France to the finals of the World Cup. He scores a penalty.
The world watches as this champion is provoked by his nemesis;
words exchanged, Achilles exposed, Zidane walks away, turns, headbutts
his tormentor in the solar plexus. We knew the anger, we knew the rage.
                    We *Black* knew the point of no return.

*

The point of no return kills. Power + Prejudice = Racism. Kriss won't fit
in any anti-racism dialogue. Tell Kriss, an innocent white boy, powerless,
kidnapped, stabbed 13 times, set alight with petrol while still alive.
Tell the activist, tell the media, tell all who would fight against racism.
                    Tell me about Kriss Donald and Ross Parker.

*

All the parts of a broken man will sink into utter darkness. Autumn leaves
falling, conkers falling, the night falling early. This man will lay in his bed,
in the dark sinking, sinking through the mattress, through the floor, descending
into earth. He's been falling a long time, flown too close to the gods, challenged all
                    and like Bruegel's 'Fall of Icarus', no one saw him fall.

*

                    He was on another journey far beyond the city, now
                    he's swallowed up in the belly of guilt and anxiety.

iii.

His head bowed heavy, images from the wall of his bedroom look down;
Janet Jackson semi-naked with her arms above her head, and from behind
a pair of hands covering her breasts. Malcolm peering through a window,
holding a rifle, and Martin quoting *We must accept finite disappointment,*
                    but never lose infinite hope.

*

It's been three days. The activist walks out in the dark rain,
midnight rain, walks canal paths, learns from the rain,
the incessant beat, beating on his head, pouring into his mind, the beauty
of being, in the darkness and glow of knowing how to love and be loved.
                    He stays out a little longer in the rain.

*

Healing comes slowly after years of being broken. He'll notice the change
in his son's voice. In his absence, one son changes from a boy to a man; another son
will never change, he'll always ask *When is dad coming home?* and a daughter
will change her father's heart to learn that every woman is somebody's daughter;
                    there's a change coming soon.

*

                    There's a knock on the door. He opens the door;
                    Dis Rasta stands and says *Physician heal thyself.*

...they killed them

Will you write about Duggan? The man wants to know. Why don't you?
Claudia Rankine

David Oluwale, 1969

~~British~~ *Wog he had no name, this*
social problem, [dirty, filthy, violent vagrant]
A quiet man, always happy, always smiling
a dangerous savage with superhuman powers.
A popular young guy, sharp dresser, excellent dancer,
menace to society, a nuisance to police, a frightening apparition.

He felt the kick between his legs, the piss that poured upon his head
by the Labour Exchange, those landlords and custodians of the law.
Kitching and Ellerker wore away the path of his mind
drove him to Middleton Woods *down in the jungle where he belonged*
and along the banks of the River Aire, Kitching and Ellerker chased him
and later that night from the River Aire they dragged his lifeless body.

On a ship named *Temple Star* from Lagos to Leeds
David Oluwale embarks on a journey of discovery.

Blair Peach, 1979

He stood up in the classroom of violence that spilled
on to streets of Southall. Playground for the bullies.
Police on foot, Police on horseback, Police heavy hand,
and he's in the thick of it, this teacher from New Zealand.

Separated from protesters, he's sitting against a garden wall.
Rescued, he's slumped in a sofa in the front room of the Atwalls.
He's lying down in the back of an ambulance.
He's dead in the theatre, a casualty of hatefulness.

Years later, his nephew is all grown up; shock
at the sight of Red Shirt protesters of Bangkok
lining the streets as he views from his office above
he grabs his camera, flies down, gets involved —

On a mobile a father implores *I lost my brother*
to a demonstration, and I don't want to lose another.

Clinton McCurbin, 1987

We moved through the city like a tide
      surging through the shopping centre
            filling and filtering into different shops
        we followed the flow and tasted fear   heaviness in the air
the moving stream whispered along and I heard *they killed him*

    the stream swelled as it curved through the mall *they killed him*
         could be clearly heard and like a pool of water dammed
ahead we tried to look above each other's heads I heard with anger said
they killed him somewhere   somehow inside of Next a man was held tight
around his neck and they never let go until he was dead

they killed him and like a swollen dam a community stood still in disbelief
spilling and pouring into evenings of disturbance   *they killed him*   We wailed
we lamented   whilst a lone voice cried out in the midst of Wolverhampton

    Babylon kill him
        Babylon kill him
            Babylon a kill we off and nobody nuh see

Orville Blackwood, 1991

He set off the fire alarm

                       And nobody came

He tore his clothes

                       And nobody came

He disrupted his care conference

                       And nobody came

He covered himself in ink

                       And nobody came

He swung for a doctor

                       And they all came

Big Black & Dangerous

                       And they all came

Injected him with a cocktail of drugs

                       And there he died.

Joy Gardner, 1993

...I couldn't believe that human beings could be so cruel to another human being,
you know it makes you quinge to hear as a mother of what they did
to my daughter in that sitting room... (they) tape up my daughter.
Public Meeting for Joy Gardner; 21st June 1995

13ft of tape,
    adhesive sticky tape,
a body belt, chains, handcuffs and tape.
    Bounded her, taped her, tied her up,
        taped her head like a mummy for the hereafter
and right here, after she ceased to breathe they made a mix-tape
    longer than any tape measure could measure.
Police, judiciary and hospital taped together
        a tapestry of events and kept a corpse alive
    until they could taper their stories to a rounded tip.
A mother is bounded by the red tape of officialdom
        until things taper off
        but a mother lights a taper in the darkness until

my tears will catch them, my tears will catch them.

Shiji Lapite, 1994

A Curtal of loss

They beat him to death? Whyyyyy? Whyyyyyy?
The wailing woman cries sitting on the floor.
Somebody in the police force killed him,
she appeals to their conscience, implores
holding her head, slapping her thighs.
Why should they kill him? Whyyyyy?

Whyyyyyy? Whyyyyy? Washes the white walls
of a police station, white faces uniformed in their silence.
She's holding her womb weighed heavy,
She's sprawled across the floor.
                         Whyyyyy? Whyyyyy?

Brian Douglas, 1995

For every atom belonging to me as good belongs to you.
Walt Whitman – 'Leaves of Grass'

THE RESULT OF POLICE ACTION, do you see it? There in the bottom right-hand corner, *'just after midnight on the morning of 3rd May 1995, Brian and his friend, Stafford Solomon, were approached by police officers... without any provocation... severe blows... administered from behind, on the back of his head.'*

> A boxing promoter in the prime of his life
> sleeping as if he was on a mission to Mars
> breathing apparatus and wires attached
> for a long journey away from this planet.
>
> In this ring he's fighting for his life
> with every atom belonging to him.
> These images that should haunt you
> won't find their way to newspaper front pages.
>
> His unshaven face cushioned in a pillow—
> the full lips of a handsome man,
> tongue relaxed as if he secretly sucked his thumb,
> eyes closed—searching for a better place.

15 hours without medical attention in Kennington Police Station. Black bodies are chased, beaten, bruised and hidden before being brought out to families, dead or in a coma. This ever-revolving door of state terror and dread.

David Bennett, 1998

As you know there are
black boys in this clinic.
I don't know if you realised
there are no Africans
on your staff at the moment.
We feel
there should be at least
two black persons
in the medical or social work staff.
For the obvious reasons
security and contentment
for all concerned
please do your best
to remedy this appalling situation.

The world's against him.
He wants to make a phone call
another patient using the phone
'black bastard, you niggers...'
Nothing is done after they fight
he feels
something should be done
to the other guy.
His sister is all that he wants
he's separated and moved
punches a female nurse in the jaw
he's pinned face down
they've released him
realising he'd stopped breathing.

Italics on the left hand side are taken from a letter David Bennett wrote to the Mental
Health Hospital.

Roger Sylvester, 1999

A High Court judge re-draws the lines
around unlawful killing to open verdict
and a brother withdraws from the system
with a bitter taste in his mouth.

Years before a Christian, a Union man
a godfather of five who'd never hurt a fly
was restrained by eight officers
never made it through the night

Notes from an officer's note book
torn out because they were defaced
these 'juvenile drawings'

covering events, time and his death
and we're to conclude there were
no sinister reasons for pages missing.

Jean Charles de Menezes, 2005

Kratos will be born out of fear and anxiety
coming alive in the midst of London bombings

inheriting the traits of Nike and Bia and Zelus
chasing after fugitives on the run looking dark like us

Zelus will ignore confirmation of said suspect
and will run with Bia from Scotia Road

with the determination of Nike and the need to protect
blindly following the man with 'Mongolian eyes'

Escaping the farms of Brazil the violence of the favellas
an electrician who came to the city of Big Ben
where opportunities ring out for hard-working men
he leaves home in the fervour of a summer day
from bus to closed station from bus to open station
he buys a newspaper walks through a ticket barrier
runs to catch the tube sitting breathless
as strangers advance towards him

And bind him by his arms on a train
And shoot him nine times in the head

Operation Kratos guidelines allowed officers to shoot without warning, since issuing a
warning could allow a potential suicide bomber to detonate a device.

Azelle Rodney, 2005

Surveillance.
Heart beating,
heart racing,
deploy, deploy.

Target acquired.
Hard stop.
Pull up
alongside.

Inhale

shot, shot, missed
third shot—in the arm; fourth shot—in the back;
fifth & sixth, double tap, military-style, through the right ear;
seventh & eighth, a brace of bullets to the vortex

Exhale.

Sean Rigg, 2008

I hope he hasn't got anything, I've got his blood on me.
He must be faking it. If there was a video, we could rewind
and find a prone man lying naked, lifeless at the feet of officers

from the cage in the yard to the cage in the van
handcuffed but moving, wedged between officers
like a carcass, face down with legs bent behind
the man will rise from the floor. If there was a video

we could rewind, he'd walk out of a police van
without being escorted, without being arrested
for theft of his own passport, which he carried
for such episodes....

He'll be waiting for hours
in a hostel, waiting for the police
to help and support. If only there was a video.

Ian Tomlinson, 2009

Minutes before you died, hands in your pocket
back turned from riot officers walking away,
you feel a strike to the leg, a push in the back
and you're suddenly launched into tomorrow's news.

There'll be headlines and photographs, footage
on YouTube after you've been helped to your feet
and you walk away seemingly unhurt, staggering
into reports and criminal investigations days later.

An *Evening Standard* vendor won't see the lies:
Police pelted with bricks as they help dying man.
Innocently you'll walk into a crowd of protesters
being *kettled* being synonymous with a new byword.

A post-mortem of your body will call of manslaughter
instead of you calling out *'Evening Standard'* on the corner.

Olaseni Lewis, 2010

A nurse warned her   not to send her child to Bethlem hospital
the place they called Bedlam   where people long ago were marked
by a star   a mother knows her child   the weight of indifference
the failure to be assured   by her son's throwaway statement
I'll be alright when I've gone to sleep   and at the rising
of a new day   she knows her son's not acting right
but there's no bed   at Maudsley   so she finds a place
for her child at Bethlem   the place   they called Bedlam
Seni hugged   staff and nurses   who told her
he could come   and go   but later refused
to let him go   staff became worried   and in the night
Seni was visited   by eleven police officers
bearing gifts   of violence and restraint   should have
left him safe   in a seclusion room   held him down
instead imagined   he was faking   left him in a coma
never to rise   on the third day   the scene of mad confusion
and a mother is forever crying   because she sent
her child to Bethlem   the place they called Bedlam

Cherry Groce, 2011

The bullet never stopped travelling,
the one that burst through her chest,
        laid her flat on her back
        whilst her son watched in shock,
                it tore through a family
                detoured to St Thomas' Hospital
                    where she laid on her back
                            fighting,
                it bounced off the minds
                of a tired community, ricocheted
                into nights of rioting, unraveling
        after leaving her paralysed
        and twenty-six years later
in the shadow of police failure
the bullet finally arrived.

Mark Duggan, 2011

He wasn't an angel, but if you are brought up in a place like the Broadwater
Farm estate, you better not be an angel because you won't survive.

– Stafford Scott, veteran community activist (Hugh Muir – Tottenham riots: *The Guardian*)

Murdered   Survived
Because there *are very few angels on Broadwater Farm*
Planning an attack   Just transporting
In possession of a firearm
One of Britain's most violent gangsters   a son, father, brother & multiple partners
being followed, tyres screeching, officers shouting
He's reaching, he's reaching   He's raising his hands holding a phone
two shots in the arm & chest   a plume of feathers filling the air
He was no angel
holding a gun, throwing it away   not holding a gun, hands held high
a gun was found on the green   nobody saw the gun fly away
the gun in the black sock
There are no angels to be found
in the shadows of the death of PC Blakelock.

Dalian Atkinson, 2016

Atkinson vs Wimbledon, (I'm a secret Villa fan)
1992, beginning of October and we're playing Wimbledon,
Dalian scoops a lofted ball out of the heavens and turns,
leaving a defender behind, with strength and guile,
skips past two players towards the penalty area,
audaciously chips a shot over a rushing goalkeeper,
rewind, slow-motion, frame by frame, play it again
repeats of *Match of the Day*, fading away.

Atkinson vs West Mercia Police, (I'm still a secret Villa fan)
2016, middle of August outside his father's house in Telford.
Dalian's pressed by officers with tasers, five shots and he's down,
they bring on the medics; kidneys and liver already gone.
This is not a game of two halves and there's no extra time,
just a family rewinding this day in slow motion, frame by frame.

Rashan Charles, 2017

A man walks into a shop followed by a police officer, moments later he dies.
A man walks into a shop, he's been walking along the well-worn paths,

over-lit with suspicions, and *you'll never amount to anything better*,
he's followed by an officer, he's thrown to the ground, struggles. He dies.

A man walks into a shop, he's followed, he's thrown to the ground, reflex or fear
he swallows something, his mouth is forced open, does it fucking matter. He dies.

A man walks into a shop wearing a cloak of survival in a world of drugs and violence,
where being black is an extra weight for young men on the streets of poverty. He dies.

A man walks into a shop I won't burden you with the weight of his twenty years
of living in a flak jacket of blackness, the need to be as swift as a basketball player
to step pass stop and search, glide past hard times. He dies.

A man walks into a shop, he's not white, headline news will make sure of that,
underline his unworthiness, label him before his body is laid down, libel him
before friends and family can speak good of him. It makes no difference. He dies.

A man walks out of a shop, notice he doesn't die. Outside a barbershop, he exchanges
the nod with elderly black men. He walks across the road to *Yo Rash what you saying?*
and he tells them it's all good. Elderly ladies laugh with him as he walks on by and
smile, *what a gentle, caring person*. He's still walking, a young girl hugs him because
he's the *guardian of the young*. Rash breaks bread with the beggars on the street, shares
the currency of time and now he rushes home to a daughter. Rash who dropped in
on the elders, *Mama P, I'm going to the shop, you want anything?* Notice he doesn't die.

Gospel According to Rasta

*I thought poetry could change everything, could change history
and could humanise, and I think that the illusion is very necessary
to push poets to be involved and to believe, but now I think
that poetry changes only the poet.*
—Mahmoud Darwish

In the city of a hundred tongues

i.

The night comes early in the city—
maybe lost, maybe on the run
but it's here to stay, it kneels and prays,
nervous in the illumination of street lamps.
Arms outstretched a barefoot Rasta stands
outside Waterstones and in a city of a hundred tongues,
in the tumult of identities, even in the din of it all,
you can find amity in this beautiful city.

ii.

Dis barefoot Rasta walked into Central Station.
Dis Rasta is swapping the sands of Morant Bay
for the brown leaves crinkling under feet.
Dis Rasta is not the famous Mutabaruka.
Dis Rasta is sitting in a Café breaking wisdom
with a writer. Dis Rasta has been travelling
a long way. Dis Rasta is he fiction or truth?

iii.

Rasta eating apple and cinnamon muffin.
Rasta: If you were to die today, what would your children
             think of you?
Writer: That's interesting; really interesting; Jeez that's interesting.
Rasta: Notice, you have repeated yourself three times.
Writer: [Silent]
Rasta: Write that down. Don't think, just write.
A writer writes, and a barefoot Rasta is walking out the door.

iv.

Standing inside Waterstones,
in between the *Good Immigrant*
and *Why I'm No Longer Talking
to White People about Race,*
the writer watches the Barefoot Rasta
standing outside with his arms outstretched.

vi.

Remember dis Rasta is not Mutabaruka.
Dis Rasta straddles histories of the
colonised and the colonialist. Dis Rasta
will not be policing state borders but
will stand in the gap in the midnight hour.
Dis Rasta will be the voice of violence
of the violated, the silence at the dawn
of revolutions. Dis Rasta will cry tears.
Dis Rasta will be seen and not seen.
Dis Rasta will at times embalm your empathy.
Dis Rasta at times will fuck up your mind.
Dis Rasta will not be found on the BBC.
Dis Rasta will be getting into your head.
Dis Rasta will not be wearing dreads
but you won't have to chase him out of town.
Dis Rasta will not be standing on corners
but will be performing from the BT Tower.

vii.

With Waterstones behind him, arms outstretched
and barefoot, a Rasta sinks into a multitude of tongues
bouncing off the soft paletes of black skies
and if all a man or a woman brings with them
is their mother tongue, in a city of a hundred tongues
we should always make room for another one.

Solomon's Love Song

But when he laid down with Makeda/ Solomon Sang/ Solomon Sang
Cassandra Wilson, *New Moon Daughter*

Dis Rasta travelled in the caravans of Makeda
to the courts of Solomon all the way from Sheba
bearing gold, jewels and spices in quantity
to discern his wisdom and popularity.

A thousand and one tales, dark and intricate sayings
they shared in the mornings and in the heat of the evenings
and when she had communed of all that was in her heart
it was he who enquired of love and sang through the night.

And Solomon and Makeda met in desire,
explored the winding streets of strong surrender
as soft sheets of night hemmed the distant horizon
where they found themselves disrobed in a new dawn.

Makeda rose and returned with the song of Solomon within her
and all the ships of Ophir couldn't fill Solomon's empty chamber.

Gods looking just like us

After we twisted and turned,
sought each other as pilgrims,
we toured into each other,
landed on drenched sheets,
lay in the vistas of our bodies,
talked about gods black and female.

I told you the powerful choose their gods,
choose how we see and believe in divinity;
if their gods are themselves re-imagined,
how could they rule if they looked like us?

The displaced have their own gods;
colour of their skin on the tip of their tongue
taking flight in a thousand languages,
a reminder of death left for another day
or a bullet hole in the shoulder
that went clean through, an oversight of God.

They carry light,
the light of the world,
the infant child born in a manger,
born running for his life.

We returned to where we left off;
kneeled and paid homage,
entered holy places and unrolled
sacred skin, revealing the divine.

No woman, no cry

after the painting by Chris Ofili

The woman in the painting towers over them head and shoulder; a chain of tears drop melodiously down her cheek and you can't help but sing *no woman, no cry*. This Nina Simonesque-braided, full-lipped, broad-nose beauty cries for the pain of motherhood. The thing that no woman should endure is the loss of her child.

The man stops because he knows the tears of his lover before they fall and sees what she sees, hears the sound pouring out of the painting; *no woman, no cry*, propped up on dung, leaning against the wall. The man sees Stephen Lawrence in the volume of tear drops, a rosary of grief held by closed eyes.

He knows the painting from articles and downloads, he knows the painting from a distance but close, the painting knows him, like all mothers know the secrets of their children before they even know.

Writings in the sky

White silence is violence

We stand shoulder to shoulder
under a canopy of pain
we make a stance
whilst police officers
watch from a distance
and pigeons flutter
waiting on the edge
of shop ledges, waiting
to hear our message.

Just because we're magic doesn't mean we're not real

We watch as young activists
make extraordinary theatre
of everyday reality
all dressed in black
tape over mouths.
We stand in silence
as a body is laid
arms outstretched
face flat to the ground.

48hrs 4 lives

Under a digital billboard
telling stories of glamour
in between stalls of religion
laying down their tales of the hereafter
and a balloon man with his own quest.
Because we have our questions too,
our déjà vu,
we begin our quest
to the sound of 'Redemption Song'

But my hand was made strong
by the hands of the Almighty

A message ripples
along the line to the heartbeat
of a drum call: 'take it off'
and tapes are ripped.
No justice, no peace
from the mouths of mothers
of babes in pushchairs,
teenagers chanting,
elders remembering.

How long shall they kill our prophets
while we stand aside and look?

Pigeons fly to the heavens
and a tired people begin their march
banners raised high like writings in the sky.

#Alton Sterling #Philando Castile #Sandra Bland #Freddie Gray
#Eric Garner #Trayvon Martin #Michael Brown #Tanisha Anderson
#Tamir Rice #Walter Scott #Sheku Bayoh #Sarah Reed #Kingsley Burrell

Conversation

Nina Simone playing in the background of a Café.

Rasta: Write it bloody and true, write the Passion of Black, write the psalms of a people, write the jazz, write the gospels, write it plain, write the protest songs from cover to cover. Illuminate the pages with love.

Writer: How do you write about the hate of centuries and not tear down and burn up? How do you write of broken lives and dead children and not give the guilty a taste of their own history or watch British rivers and canals filled with pale berries?

Rasta: Listen, shhhh, listen...

Nina: *I wish I could share all the love in my heart / I wish I could break all things that bind us apart*

Rasta: Listen, ping-ping, (*like he was playing a piano*)

Nina: *Wish you could know what it means to be me / Then you'd see, you'd agree, everybody should be free.*

Rasta: You hear dat? That's what you feeling. Write it, carry it. I want you to carry it wherever you go, carry it under your arm, under your pillow, carry it for another hundred years. No, a thousand years until there's no more crying, no more sorrows, until every man of colour carries the load, until we carry his load, her load, together I'n'I carrying freedom in the breath that we breathe.

Writer: And what about Stephen, Joy, Mark, Anthony, Rashan. Not one of them is called Lazarus! After all the inquest, all the post mortems, all the police inquiries, nobody's found guilty for all of that shit.

Rasta: That's what you write, the ping-ping, the rise and flow, the silence, the violence, the vibrato and whatever they call it and then sing it. We are the disciples who beareth witness of these things so write, write it all.

Dancing with Ghosts

Our mothers prayed before a God with three names,
danced with a ghost from Pentecost,
spoke in tongues and believed in the magic
of another world where ancestors danced with the spirit.

They were mothers that needed the hurt to be loved away,
needed to be loved in the absence of lovers.
The spirit entered you, loved you, caused you to buck
and wail, loved you like you'd never been loved before.

We learned to dance like our mothers of the church,
round, thin, dark, light, those with pride
who could barely talk to you and those who hugged you with love,
full breasts that absorbed you, warm bodies wrapped around you.

We danced like they did, we who had been
fed on verses and chapters from birth
and those who were new, wide-eyed
and eager to be loved, we danced to midnight
with ghosts we barely knew, went to school
the next day with kids who spoke of Lovers Rock,
shubeen and midnight dances in front rooms.

Our mothers danced at morning prayers,
noon-time singing and evening revivals.
Danced in high heels, barefoot
danced in short dresses.
Danced at births and funerals,
even the birth of Christ,
and his death too.

Their hands

Trying to fashion a world that will hold all the people, all the faces,
all the adams and eves and their countless generations
—Margaret Walker, *For My People*

Their hands loved and caressed, cajoled the fears out of lonely nights,
       fed men with hope and washed the indignity off their faces
       and in the cold morning would unwrap themselves from men
       who'd venture another day into fogs of uncertainties.

Their hands worked too. Worked in mills and factories,
       mopped floors, fed people, cut cords of the newborn
       worked day and night for pay packets that weighed
       less than those called Mary and Jane.

Their hands knew change, change in their bodies, seasons
       of blood that ceased, the beginning of life and in those times
       found God, lost God, loved God, became gods bringing life
       into this world and sometimes cried in the twilight of stillbirth.

Their hands have brushed the dust of hate from paths and doorsteps,
       scrubbed hallways clean of the ignorance of others but sometimes
       bitter blood seeps from outside and anger boils over from generation
       to generation, turning hands into clenched rage on the eve of riots.

Their hands have lost the gloss of youth, are loose with veins like
       tree roots bursting to the surface, some creaking painfully,
       some twisted, knuckles thickened, others shaking violently,
       others holding on to memories in the dirges of *dust to dust.*

Their hands are the hands of women who loved freedom. Hands
       that tried to make a new world from patchwork quilts
       soft enough to lay down and rest on, large enough to cover
       all the people and strong enough to hold us all together.

Arms outstretched

Dis Rasta, arms outstretched
chained to rocks, rough iron holds
him who dared to defy the Gods,
to break their grip, to question their stories,
and sight something new, something beautiful
that begins within and heals without.

Dis Rasta dreadlock Christ hung on a tree,
him blood run down across centuries, from where
the state jook him up and the righteous stand up and watch
him sweat, tears and lifewater flow to bless and heal
beyond borders of politricks, hypocrites and murderers—
for as much as you did unto them you did unto me.

Dis Rasta is the thousands of women beaten,
arms outstretched, pleading for mercy
before tied to drowning chairs, the innocent
to die by water and the witches survive
to burn in fires set by devils wrapped in cloaks
of man fear and a god that looked like them.

Dis Rasta walked with Paul Bogle and hundreds more
to Morant Bay to drive buckra back a England.
Dis Rasta fight with head, heart, rockstone and cutlass
but had to run as militia opened fire and cut them down like cane.
Dis Rasta run go hide in the hills. Six hundred get whipped to the bone
and four hundred more hang and fly away home.

Dis Rasta is running from the hills with limbs
harvested by Leopold and walking ghetto streets barefoot
after Kristallnacht wearing David's star,
Dis Rasta rose from the oven-ash of holocaust,
climbing from under the bones of genocide
only to change garments with Palestinians.

Dis Rasta is a shadow left on the playgrounds
of Hiroshima, arms outstretched, against a red sky
running to waters filled with bodies, bloated horses
and black rain, black rain everywhere.
Dis Rasta is running for his life, her life, life
running from atrocity to atrocity.

Dis Rasta is a child, dead, curled up on a beach
picked up by the outstretched arms of a stranger.

A British thing to do

standing in queues; queues
appear out of nowhere
and disappear; queues
are filled with weathers
and gossip; queues bulge
ahead with best mates
and family; queues will have
the annoying kid screaming
and twisting; queues
will be coloured with tuts
and intakes of frustration
and always *I'm running late*
conversations on mobiles.
Queues are always held up
by the man with change
scattered across the counter
or the woman with a list
of needs and one last
thought to share. Queues
may have the occasional
lovers lost in each other
or the lover walking away
lost in disbelief. Queues
of apologies of *I'll be quick*
and the one behind shouting
what the hell is holding up this line?
Queues that begin on Boxing
Day and end on the opening
of New Year sales; queues
inside and outside buildings,
straight around corners.
And there's always *is this*
why we fought two bloody
world wars, to be over-
run by bloody foreigners?

Gabay of hope

Here under heaven in this hour let us breathe hope into a new millennium, let us
believe in the humanity of others, let us harbour all that is honorable and heavenly

  Breathe   Heaven is here, this hour, right now; let not the haves
rob the have-nots of their heavenly moment here on earth, sowing seeds of separation.

Here under heaven we are the sum total of earth, air and water, alive with the fire
which ignites the living soul. However abled, we are heavenly bodies,

sweet smelling herbs. We are the harmony of faith and healing. *Breathe*
We are the hallelujah, the hosanna, the hymn that heralds a bright new morning.

Here under heaven this very hour we walk upon hallowed ground, hewn out
of humanity's aspirations for greater things, written in henna on the back

of our hands, forever a halo above our heads the alliteration of hope. Let our bodies
be a Hajj, until we become the Hanukkah of the night and the Halcyon of days.

Liberty

Love begins at home and not all homes have wallpaper, lace curtains, or doors oiled and door steps scrubbed every day. Love bears the heaviest burdens but light to carry. Love is

> *You're a married man now, son,*
>> *do the best you can, love God*
>>> *and these doors will always be open.*

Love breathes in the months of absence, too busy to visit, too engrossed to call, travelling around the world or creating your own little world. Love is that mango tree that grew in the yard back in Jamaica, growing across oceans, growing in front rooms, protected and watered, growing a thick head of green afro, heavy with love. Love that grew in seasons of winter where a husband and father was lost. Love that gnarled and twisted around failings.

> *You know the difference between right and wrong*

but still holding a son in the centre of her eyes, holding a son all broken-winged and asking *What you want to eat son?* And for months, a son will stay in the mango tree too broken-winged to fly, no voice to sing, but a mother will climb the tree, sit next to her son and stretch out to catch a mango falling because mangoes fall freely; because in devouring the flesh, turning skin inside out, a sweetness will perfume the air; because she will cut it into thirds, avoiding the heart.

The beginning of love

is when the volume's turned down

and we listen to the wings

of a ladybird as it becomes aware

of the fall of a leaf—

we eavesdrop on the discourse

between the night and the dawn

and we're carried away

on the breath of a new day.

Now is the time for healing—

Notes

New Millennium Journal

'1999 – Parts of a broken man': The Stephen Lawrence Inquiry, otherwise known as the MacPherson Report, was a turning point in race relations at the turn of the millennium. This landmark report detailed the events leading up to the brutal racially-motivated attack upon Stephen Lawrence that led to his death. The report also found that the Metropolitan Police was institutionally racist, providing a way forward with seventy recommendations for reform.

... they killed them

The Hounding of David Oluwale, Kester Aspden (Vintage Publishing, 2008).

Deadly Silence: Black Deaths in Custody, edited by A. Sivanandan (Institute of Race Relations, 1991).

Dying for Justice, edited by Harmit Athwal and Jenny Bourne (Institute of Race Relations, 2015).

Lawful Killing: Mark Duggan (2016). Docudrama about the police shooting of Mark Duggan in Tottenham, North London in August 2011.

Justice Denied: A film about Joy Gardner who died in 1993 after police officers and deportation officers restrained her using a body belt, ankle straps and gagging her mouth with thirteen feet of tape.

Who Polices the Police?: A documentary about the flawed investigation by the IPCC into the death of Sean Rigg whilst in police custody.

Injustice: A film documenting the struggles of families of people who have died in police custody. http://www.injusticefilm.co.uk.

Friends of Mikey Powell Campaign for Justice:
http://mikeypowell-campaign.org.uk

4WardEverUk: http://4wardeveruk.org

Inquest: http://www.inquest.org.uk/about/home

United Family and Friends Campaign: https://uffcampaign.org/

Migrant Media: Migrant media is a group of political film-makers

Gospel According to Rasta

'Gabay of Hope' is influenced by the traditional Somali poetic form called the gabay. The form is made of long lines, stretched over long verse paragraphs and uses alliteration through its form. I'm grateful to Asha Lul Mohamud Yusuf, and her book *The Sea-Migrations: Tahriib* (Bloodaxe Books, 2017), translated by Clare Pollard.

Thanks and Acknowledgements

Gratitude to the following for the temporary home given to many of my poems that have appeared, sometimes in different forms:

'Dancing with Ghosts' in *Filligree* (Peepal Tree, 2018); 'A British thing to do' in *Why Poetry? Lunar Poetry Podcasts* (Verve Poetry Press 2018); 'In The City of a Hundred Tongues' in *It All Radiates Outwards* (Verve Poetry Press 2018); '1999 – Parts of a Broken Man' in *Somewhere to keep the rain* (Winchester Poetry Festival, 2017); 'Their Hands' commissioned for Freedom in the City, National Poetry Day (Writing West Midlands 2017); 'The Beginning of Love', a collaborative experimental poem with Linda Kemp for *Disonance* (Hesterglock Press 2017)

A whole heap of thanks to The Poetry School & Newcastle University; Tamar Yoseloff especially who introduced me to Jill McDonough, Habeaus Corpus and the countless hours ruminating over Claudia Rankine. Also not forgetting Clare Pollard, Glyn Maxwell, John Canfield & Tara Bergin for pushing and challenging me to write my truth and special mention to my peers Elaine, Lauren, Iulia, Barbara, Sarah & Greg.

Special mention for Harmit Athwal for the close working relationship, advice, indepth knowledge and access to files on death in custody amassed over the years of the Institute for Race Relations' existence. Special thanks to Liz Fekete and Colin Prescod for their moral support.

I'm indebted to everyone who helped me along the way with this second collection including all my family—Myles, Matthew and Nina; and friends, especially Paul Grant, Phillip Simpson, Ruby Robinson, & Predencia, my inner circle of creativity. Suzanne Iuppa for a place to retreat to in the middle of Wales. Ita Gooden, Mic Fever & the Mango Lounge for the love and support. Writing West Midlands, Jonathan Davidson & Wolverhampton City Voices, Simon Fletcher for the early days. Stuart Bartholomew & Cynthia Miller for the stage and the page to shine. Thank you to artist Barbara Walker for the permission to use her artwork on the cover of this book.

And give thanks to Jane for her belief, love and grace shown to me and my collection. And finally to Maish and Kaleigh for being there through my illness and loving me in my darkest hours.